Text © 2008 by Janet Severi Bristow and
Victoria A. Cole-Galo
Photographs © 2008 by Tom Hopkins Photography
Illustrations © 2008 by Christine Erikson
The Taunton Press, Inc.

This material was previously published in the book
*The Prayer Shawl Companion 38 Knitted Designs to
Embrace Inspire & Celebrate Life*
(ISBN 978-1-60085-003-5)
First published in this format 2012

The Taunton Press, Inc., 63 South Main Street,
PO Box 5506, Newtown, CT 06470-5506
e-mail: tp@taunton.com

Interior Design: Kimberly Adis
Illustrator: Christine Erickson
Photographer: Tom Hopkins Photography,
Wendy Mijal

Threads® is a trademark of The Taunton Press, Inc.,
registered in the U.S. Patent and Trademark Office.

The following names/manufacturers appearing in
Knitted Prayer Shawls are trademarks: Alchemy™,
Bernat®, Caron®, Caron® Perfect Match®,
Jo Ann™ Sensations™, Patons®, Red Heart®
Soft Yarn™

Printed in the United States of America
10 9 8 7 6 5 4 3 2 1

CONTENTS

BEGINNING PRAYERFULLY

PRAYER SHAWLS BECOME TANGIBLE SYMBOLS OF LOVE WHEN words can't be found to adequately express one's feelings. They can be warm hugs of happiness, empathy, and support; a private place of escape in which to rest, relax, and renew; something to hold on to when all else seems to be slipping away. Wrapping another in a shawl knit of your own prayers and loving thoughts is a gift not only for the one receiving the shawl but for yourself as well. Here we'll show you how to turn your shawl making into an experience that blesses everyone involved.

Prayer begins in the heart. Because the creation of a prayer shawl is, first, a spiritual practice for the shawl maker, it's important to set an environment of intention, or purpose, as you begin.

Thinking about Who Will Wear the Shawl

The first step in establishing intention occurs when you hear of a need or are inspired to reach out to another person in his or her time of difficulty or celebration—a family member, friend, neighbor, acquaintance, or even someone you've never met but heard about from others. We encourage you to "trust the shawl." It will go to just the right person and arrive at just the right time. Often enough, it happens that when we start out knitting a shawl with a particular person in mind, a more urgent need arises and someone else needs it even more. Or there are times when we begin a shawl with no recipient in mind, believing that the person who needs it will eventually come into our lives. Once you get started, we have no doubt that you will find this to be true for you, too.

Choosing Yarn

When we begin knitting any project for another person, we plan it with that person in mind. What are the recipient's favorite colors? What fiber will feel best against his or her skin? When we choose yarn for a prayer shawl, the process is no different. Whether you know the recipient of your shawl or not, consider first the color or colors you will use, as they will have an effect on the recipient. Bright colors such as red or gold generally uplift and energize, as seen in

Alice's Lace Shawl (page 28); dark colors often give a sense of escape and enfolding, as they do in the Traveling Shawl (page 26). And as illustrated by the Nursing Shawl (page 21), neutrals and pastels tend to be comforting. Once you've chosen the colors, trust your selection—it will be right for the person who receives it.

Next, consider the type of yarn you will use. If you're making a shawl with an intricate pattern or are knitting for someone with simple taste, you might prefer a smooth, worsted-weight yarn to emphasize the design. When the pattern is plain and texture is the focus, you may wish to use a knobby bouclé or other type of novelty yarn. Higher-end yarns, such as hand-painted yarns and those made with luxury fibers, may be desired for very special shawls, perhaps one intended for a dear friend. Some shawl makers use remnants of yarn—mixing colors, types, and textures—to create dramatic, one-of-a-kind shawls known as Joseph's coat shawls, oddball shawls, gypsy shawls, patchwork shawls, or *anawim* shawls (a Hebrew word meaning "God's faithful remnant"). The Traveling Shawl (page 26) is a beautiful example. Once you're comfortable with the shawl-making process, we encourage you to experiment with color, pattern, and yarn. Allow yourself to be inspired, express your creativity, and enjoy the experience.

Creating the Environment

You may not realize it, but everything we've talked about up to now is part of the spiritual experience of making a shawl. Of course, the actual knitting is much more intensely spiritual, so it's important to take the time to set the mood. In doing so, consider creating a small ritual that is meaningful to you. Here are a few suggestions that have worked nicely for us.

Before you sit down to begin, gather together:

- Yarn
- Tools
- Candle and matches
- Journal and pen
- Favorite prayer, poem, or reading

You may also wish to have the following:

- Mild scented hand lotion (unless your shawl recipient is sensitive to smells or allergic to such products)
- Something to drink (perhaps a cup of tea)
- Music (a favorite CD or a radio station that plays soothing or meditative music)

Find a quiet spot and get comfortable. The ideal is away from the TV in a peaceful place either inside or outside. Then, begin as follows:

- Sit quietly for a moment.
- Take a few deep breaths to relax.
- Center yourself and reflect on what you're about to do.

- Light the candle and massage the lotion into your hands to prepare them for the task ahead.
- Record the date in your journal and, as you knit, jot down insights, thoughts, and reflections that come to you. You may wish to include these in a note you give to the person who receives your shawl; they might also be the beginnings of a prayer, blessing, or poem. Some groups that co-knit a shawl keep a journal of their collective experience and include the journal with the shawl when it's given away.
- Place your hand on the yarn, recite a blessing, read a poem or prayer, or just sit quietly for a moment.
- If you've chosen music, play it softly in the background.
- Begin casting on your stitches.

As you work, think about or pray for the person who will receive your shawl. Remember being swaddled in a blanket as a child. Recall the feeling of utter bliss and complete surrender when being enfolded by someone who cares for you. Pray those memories into your knitting along with thoughts of strength, peace, and healing for the one who will receive the work of your hands. Make this process an extension of your life and the desires of your heart. Rest assured that the energy you impart will be felt. Usually, you will take your time making a shawl, finding bits of time in your day when you can calmly and prayerfully work on it. Sometimes you'll work in solitude, but you may often find yourself weaving the pattern of your life into the pattern of the shawl as it accompanies you to meetings, appointments, soccer games, and gatherings.

You'll find that folks are interested in what you're doing. As you explain, little seeds of interest are planted (and so the ministry grows). Of course, there may be occasions when you need to speed up the shawl-making process. We have found that emergency situations—such as accidents, urgent surgeries, or a sudden death—can sometimes cut short the time we thought we had to work on a shawl, so we'll enlist a few friends or our group to help, passing the work from one person to another.

Adding Embellishment

After you've finished the body of the shawl, you may decide to embellish it with fringe or tassels. This too can be an occasion for prayer. Some people tie a knot into various pieces of fringe as they work, keeping the intentions of the receiver in mind or saying a prayer for her or him as they do. Members of some Prayer Shawl Ministry groups take turns tying a knot in each others' shawls to add their prayers, as well.

Charms and beads also add to a shawl's beauty and can be a source of meditation. Hearts, angels, and religious symbols are popular choices, but consider others. If you know the recipient of the shawl, you can add some significant symbols or colorful beads that connect the two of you. For example, add a flower charm if you both enjoy gardening or a seashell if you share a love of the ocean.

If the shawl is a gift from a group, invite everyone to add his or her own tokens of affection and remembrances. Encourage recipients to add beads or charms of their own, perhaps something that belonged to family members or friends. A locket with a picture of a loved one is a personal touch as well. If the recipient is Catholic, then adding 10 beads to each side of the shawl would enable the wearer to say a few decades of the rosary.

Blessing the Shawl

When the shawl is completed, offer up a final blessing before it is sent on its way. If you belong to a group, gather around the finished shawl, lay your hands on it, and say a blessing in unison. Some groups bless their shawls once a month in church. This is a great way to include the members of the congregation who don't knit or crochet. You or your group may wish to write your own blessing, or you may choose a favorite poem, prayer, or benediction. You can get lots of ideas from our website (www.shawlministry.com).

Then, before you give the shawl away, think about what words you'd like to include with it. Revisit your journal and, if you wish, attach a note, tag, or card that answers the following questions:

- What is a prayer shawl?
- Why has the shawl been given away?
- Who is giving the shawl?

Each person or group may decide what to say to a shawl's recipient. Some groups write detailed letters to explain the meanings of the color and other symbolism (such as the number of stitches in the pattern or the significance of the charms added) along with a blessing. Sometimes a tag with a blessing is tied to the fringe; occasionally, groups special-order cloth labels that identify the group or organization and are sewn onto a corner of the shawl. Or you may simply include a handwritten, from-the-heart card.

Presenting a Shawl

Depending on the circumstances, there are many ways of presenting a shawl. If you are delivering a shawl by yourself and in person, you may simply give the shawl to the one it's intended for, explaining what it is and why you want her or him to have it. If you feel comfortable, consider saying a little blessing, prayer, or poem as you drape the shawl around the person's shoulders. Don't worry if the person doesn't seem as receptive as you'd

like—sometimes it takes a while for it all to sink in. This might become an opportunity for quiet conversation, reflection, or even shared tears. What's most important is that it is a sacred moment in which the giver, the receiver, and others present are blessed.

This is not as easy as it sounds for many of us. We may feel uncomfortable or awkward around others who are in pain or experiencing grief. What are we supposed to say? What if we say the wrong thing? What if we unintentionally cause the person more pain? It's normal to worry about these things. But you don't have to know all the right words to make this a meaningful moment. Your very presence, your willingness to listen, and your shawl will be enough. If the person receiving the shawl begins to cry, or even wishes to talk, simple responses such as nodding, touching a hand or shoulder, asking a specific question or two, or making a small comment to show you are listening are entirely appropriate. Listening and simply being present with the person are the best gifts you can offer.

If a group of friends are presenting the shawl, it's lovely to have the recipient stand (if possible) or sit in the middle of the group, then have everyone place a hand on the shawl as you read the blessing in unison. Our first shawl, for a friend going through a divorce, was presented in this manner. We gathered together a group of sister friends, each of us taking turns wrapping up in the shawl and sharing a blessing, either spoken aloud or silently in our hearts. As it was wrapped around our friend's shoulders, she was told of the prayers and good wishes that had been prayed into it by those who cared for her.

Always let the circumstances, the place, and the personality of the person who is to receive your shawl be your guide. What we've described is a wonderful opportunity of sharing and blessing for all involved. Make sure there is enough time for this ritual.

On the other hand, there will be occasions when you won't be involved in a formal presentation. Sometimes shawls are picked up by family members or friends, or they're sent by mail. However the shawl is received, trust that it will be a sacred moment, and one that happens at just the right time.

Finally, regardless of how the wrap is presented, there are a few things to keep in mind when packaging a shawl for presentation and delivery. Here are some ideas for packaging your shawls in an attractive—but practical—manner:

• Place it in a 2-gallon sealable plastic bag. These are especially handy for less personal deliveries to hospitals, nursing homes, and so on. They are easy to store and hold everything you wish to include with the shawl, such as tags, letters, cards, and sachets.

• Place it in a decorative gift bag when you're giving someone his or her shawl in person. Gift bags, though less durable, can also hold other items you'd like to include.

• Hand sew, knit, or crochet a pouch from remnants of fabric or yarn. This type of bag creates a little pillow when the shawl is stored in it.

• Simply wrap the shawl in pretty tissue paper, wrapping paper, or fabric, tied with a piece of yarn.

Receiving a Shawl

All prayer shawl makers are eager to be givers, but we encourage you to allow yourself to be a willing recipient as well, if the occasion arises. There's a certain amount of letting go in allowing someone else to minister to you, and this can be a welcome relief to a shawl maker who is always on the giving end. We hope the time comes when someone gives you a shawl so that you may welcome the full-circle blessings of being both giver and receiver.

Gentle Shawl Making

Gentle shawl making is how we describe less physically demanding knitting practices for those of us with health issues that impede our knitting—carpal tunnel syndrome, fibromyalgia, arthritis, and others. If knitting is physically difficult for you, but you'd still like to participate in the Prayer Shawl Ministry, start simply, slowly, and prayerfully. Do what you can in small blocks of time, putting the work aside when you need a rest. You may want to do just part of a shawl and pass it on to someone else. Or you could prayerfully concentrate on the fringe or border of a shawl that someone else has made. The most important component of this ministry is prayer, which doesn't require any physical strength, just a desire of the heart.

If you would like to make prayer shawls, but are hesitant to do so because of health concerns, please reconsider. We have received inspiring e-mails from shawl makers with health challenges who say that being involved in this ministry helps them focus on others, remain active, and stay connected to their faith community. Their shawl-making process may have its limits, but the benefits are limitless.

W E SUGGEST THIS PATTERN FOR FIRST-TIME

FROM
Victoria A. Cole-Galo
& Rosann Guzauckas
Wethersfield, Connecticut

knitters—it's made with knit stitches only, known as the Garter Stitch. The same effect can be achieved with all purl stitches, too—a fun way to master the purl stitch if it's new to you. Once you are comfortable with either stitch, you're ready to begin making a prayer shawl. Also, several shawl makers have told us they made their first shawl for someone who has or had cancer. The shawl pictured here was made in pink—the symbolic color of breast cancer survivors.

BEGINNER'S SHAWL

Skill Level
Easy

Finished Measurements
76 in long and 19 in wide

Yarn
• Bulky Weight Yarn (CYCA 5), approx 850 yd lightweight bouclé yarn
• Shawl shown in Jo-Ann™ Sensations™ Rainbow Bouclé (88% acrylic/13% nylon; 853 yd/11 oz), 1 skein Light Pink

Needles
• Size 10½ straight or circular needles (or size needed to obtain gauge)

Gauge
• 16 sts and 22 rows = 4 in worked in Garter Stitch

Note: This shawl can easily be made any size and with any yarn. When choosing yarn, refer to "Standard Yarn Weights," on page 31. This will give you an indication of how much yarn you will need as well as what size needle. We recommend using large needles (size 10½ to size 15) and thick yarns for this type of shawl. You can use medium-weight yarns with large needles, too—the shawl will appear lacy. We do not recommend using small needles with thick yarn.

DIRECTIONS
CO 68 sts. Knit every row until shawl measures 76 in, or desired length. BO.

IN WHOLENESS
AND HEALTH

As this shawl is knit together with prayer, may your body and soul be again knit together in wholeness and health.

—THE REVEREND REBECCA SEGERS
PRESBYTERIAN CHURCH OF SWEET HOLLOW
MELVILLE, NEW YORK

Light and Healing

No words can describe the loss I felt when my 12-day-old grandson, Garrett James Denslaw, died.

One day at my knitting group, a woman brought information about the Prayer Shawl Ministry. Not long after, a close friend in the group presented me with a beautiful shawl.

At home, I wrapped my shawl around me and allowed myself to cry and grieve the loss of my grandson. Slowly, I sensed that healing was taking place within me. I hoped someday I would be able to knit prayer shawls for others who were hurting.

The following year I was knitting prayer shawls. I always attach fringe, and sometimes I include a small silver heart charm.

Most of the shawls I knit are to offer comfort to people. Recently I began knitting shawls to celebrate the joys in life. Once the recipients wrap the shawl around themselves, they understand the meaning of the ministry.

As I look back, I can see that the Prayer Shawl Ministry provided direction, light, and healing on my journey of grief. This has been a true blessing in my life.

SUSAN ALLGAIER, Wixom, Michigan

THIS SHAWL IS A METAPHOR FOR FRIENDSHIP. In keeping with the symbolism of threes, it is made with three stitches. Garter Stitch is a dependable, basic stitch. Stockinette Stitch is a mainstay, combining the smooth knitted stitch on one side and the bumpier purl on the other. Seed Stitch takes time and focus. We all have friends who fit these categories. Each one is unique and treasured. This shawl is very adaptable in that the shawl maker can use any color and type of yarn, or three stitch types. The multiple strands are knit together, symbolizing the friendship two people share, but the shawl can be made with a single strand as long as the needle size is adjusted to fit the yarn.

FROM
Janet Severi Bristow

FRIENDSHIP PATCHWORK SHAWL

Skill Level
Easy

Finished Measurements
60 in long and 20 in wide

Yarn
Note: This amount of yarn will make two shawls—enough to share with a friend. If you wish to make only one shawl, simply divide the required yarn amounts in half.
- 500 yd Medium Weight Yarn (CYCA 4) (Color A)
- 500 yd Medium Weight Yarn (CYCA 4) (Color B)
- 750 yd Bulky Weight Yarn (CYCA 5) bouclé yarn
- 60 yd Bulky Weight Yarn (CYCA 5) novelty yarn

- Shawl shown in Caron® Simply Soft (100% acrylic; 330 yd/6 oz), 2 skeins #9738 Violet; Red Heart® Soft Yarn™ (100% acrylic; 256 yd/5 oz), 2 skeins #9537 Fuchsia; Bernat® Soft Bouclé (97% acrylic/3% polyester; 255 yd/5 oz), 3 skeins #26960 Crazy Shades; Patons® Carmen (36% polyester/64% nylon; 64 yd/1.75 oz), 1 skein #07310 Violet

Needles
- Size 17 or 19 straight or circular needles (or size needed to obtain gauge)

Gauge
- 10 sts and 10 rows = 4 in worked in Stockinette Stitch
- 14 sts and 12 rows = 4 in worked in Garter Stitch
- 10 sts and 14 rows = 4 in worked in Seed Stitch

FRIENDSHIP PATCHWORK SHAWL

DIRECTIONS

Note: Row numbers are approx. Feel free to adjust number of rows you knit with the different yarn combinations.

With 2 strands Color A and 1 strand novelty yarn held tog, CO on 43 sts or number for desired width (being sure number of sts is odd).

Row 1: Knit across.

Rows 2–9: Drop novelty yarn. With 2 strands Color A, knit all rows (Garter Stitch).

Row 10: Drop Color A. With 2 strands Color B, k1, p1 across (Seed Stitch).

Rows 11–16: Knit the purl sts and purl the knit sts as they face you.

Rows 17–29: Drop Color B. With 2 strands bouclé, knit all odd rows and purl all even rows (Stockinette Stitch).

Continue working Rows 1–29, adding novelty yarn for 2 rows whenever you choose, until shawl measures approx 60 in. **Note:** Length of shawl can be wrist-to-wrist or fingertip-to-fingertip, if desired.

BO all sts and add fringe using 16-in strands of each yarn for each fringe as follows: 1 strand novelty, 2 strands bouclé, and 2 strands each of Colors A and B.

FRINGE

Cut yarn to the length specified in pattern, or twice the length of desired fringe (for example, cut 16-in lengths for an 8-in fringe). Holding together as many lengths as desired, fold the lengths in half, insert a crochet hook into the first stitch on either the cast-on or bound-off edge of the shawl, pull up a loop by catching the lengths of fringe at their center point and pulling the loose ends through the loop. Pull to tighten. Repeat across the edge. Trim the fringe even, if necessary.

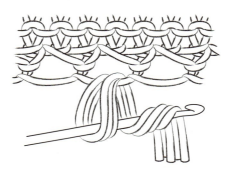

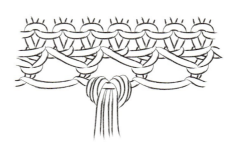

Soul Sisters

Jeanette came into my life as a special gift from the Creator. She was my soul mate and a spiritual companion. She battled with cancer, and as she did, she taught me how to live daily in grace-filled moments. Jeanette saw God working in every dimension of her life, whether she was listening to her favorite music, working in her flower garden, or preparing meals for her family. The ability to listen to others was the fuel that brought her calm and enlightenment.

When we visited, we prayed and wrapped ourselves in our prayer shawls, their fringes tangling together as we held hands. We spoke about our spiritual experiences, and we admired the special beads and symbols attached to the fringes of our shawls, including some she had received from her daughters, Laura and Alice, and her grandchildren. The fringe also included a handmade signet ring from her father-in-law. All these items gave Jeanette the feeling of a deep spiritual connectedness with her loved ones. Each of our shawls also had a decade of the rosary that I had added to the fringes, so we could finger the beads as we prayed Hail Marys. This ritual filled us with tranquility and courage, even as we shared our inner thoughts and cried,

knowing her beautiful journey of life would come to an end much too quickly. Our prayer shawls had created a unique and lasting bond between two like-minded women.

One day, Jeanette asked me if the prayer shawl I had knitted so prayerfully and lovingly for her could be used as her burial shroud. Without hesitation, I agreed. When the end of her life arrived, her husband, Anthony, gave instructions that Jeanette's prayer shawl be laid out to cover her from head to foot. With this act, we felt that the shawl had been transformed into the arms of the Lord, embracing Jeanette and guiding her to meet all the loved ones who had passed before her.

Death does not separate soul sisters. Those we knit shawls for are never at a distance because we remember that this unassuming act of love—knitting for another—can have great power in our lives. The secret is to teach ourselves to stay present to the moment, to knit *for* the person, known or unknown. The knitting of a prayer shawl is truly a gift, a positive action that can be shared with those we encounter in our daily world. I have abundant daily reminders of Jeanette, and in them, ever so slightly, the fringes of our shawls seem to touch each other once again.

GLADYS COLE, Nokomis, Florida

THESE TWO SHAWLS ARE SMALLER VERSIONS OF THE ORIGINAL
prayer shawl pattern, based on the knit three, purl three pattern. They can be used
as baby gifts or knitted for baptisms, christenings, or baby naming ceremonies.
They may also be given to any child as a source of comfort and solace. The first
pattern is by Janet Severi Bristow and the second is from Susan Meader Tobias.

BAPTISM SHAWLS

FROM
Janet Severi
Bristow

Rectangle Baptism Shawl

Skill Level
Easy

Finished Measurements
31 in long and 13 in wide (without edging)

Yarn
• Medium Weight Yarn (CYCA 4), approx 350 yd variegated
• Shawl shown in Caron® Perfect Match® (100% acrylic; 355 yd/7 oz), 1 skein #7401 Baby Rainbow Ombre

Needles
• Size 10 straight or circular needles (or size needed to obtain gauge)
• Size G crochet hook (optional)

Gauge
• 15 sts and 25 rows = 4 in worked in k3, p3 pattern

DIRECTIONS
CO 21 or 24 sts, or number for desired width (number of sts must be a multiple of 3).

Row 1: K3, p3 across.

Row 2: Knit the purl sts and purl the knit sts as they face you.

Work as established until shawl is 31 in or desired length. BO all sts.

FINISHING
Add fringe (see page 14) or crochet a simple ch-st edging, as follows: Attach yarn in one corner of shawl with a sc, *ch 5, sk 1 st, work 1 sc in next st, repeat from * around shawl.

FROM
Susan Meader
Tobias
Washington, D.C.

Triangle Baptism Shawl

Skill Level
Easy

Finished Measurements
45 in long and 20 in deep

Yarn
- Medium Weight Yarn (CYCA 4) approx 180 yd yellow
- Shawl not shown.

Needles
- Size 13 straight or circular needle (or size needed to obtain gauge)

Notions
- Stitch markers

Gauge
- 12 sts and 14 rows = 4 in worked in 3-St Pattern

DIRECTIONS
CO 3 sts.

Row 1: Inc 1 st in each st. (6 sts)

Row 2: K3, p3 across.

Rows 3–99: Inc 1 st at beginning of every row, maintaining the 3-St Pattern by purling the knits and knitting the purls as they face you. You may need to use markers to help keep track of the 3-st repeats, because each row will be different.

BO loosely.

WE KNIT

We take up our needles and yarn . . .
And . . . we knit.
God took earth, sea, and sky
To create this world.
He knitted it all together, and . . .
Said, "It is good."

We knit . . . stitch by stitch . . .
To create a garment of love.
God's love surrounds us as
We knit . . . and pray.

Row by row, and prayer by prayer,
In a pattern of threes . . . we knit . . .
God, the Son, the Holy Spirit.
Elizabeth, Mary, Martha . . .
Women of faith who have led the way.

Melodies quiet the soul and dismiss all stress,
As we knit.
The knitting continues and becomes a shawl
To be a wrapping
Of love, compassion, and togetherness.

Embellished with fringe,
And blessed by the group.
It is presented as a token of care and concern,
Compassion or celebration.
Love embraces, encourages, sustains . . .
And the circle of love is complete.

"I was naked and you clothed me,
I was sick and you visited me . . .
As you did it to the least of these my brethren,
You did it unto me."

—MYRTLE L. COUNCIL
SHILLINGTON, PENNSYLVANIA

Pink Shawls for Two

One day I received a call from the pastor of our congregation asking if I could quickly make a baby shawl. Prayers were needed for a newborn who had been born prematurely.

I think God had known this request would be coming. Some time before this, I had started a pink shawl. I knew I had only enough yarn to knit about half of the usual 6-ft length of a prayer shawl, but I didn't worry about that because this was "no-dye-lot" yarn, and I could go back and get another matching skein at any time. No such luck. I carried a piece of the yarn with me for months, checking every store I went into, but the new yarns were all a bit darker. So my half-done shawl lay in my knitting basket until that phone call telling me of the new baby who had come so early. I picked up the pink in-process shawl, ripped out a few rows to get enough yarn for the fringe, and was able to finish the baby-size shawl in just one day.

Shortly after this, another tiny baby girl was born. This time, I knitted another little pink prayer shawl from scratch. And now, almost 2 years later, these two tiny babies have grown to be beautiful, energetic little girls who run around our church halls. The blessings in these shawls have returned to us many-fold.

Seeing a shawl being blessed is very rewarding; I feel its warmth as if it were around my shoulders. Being a part of this ministry that is not so quiet anymore and seeing it grow from person to person is very special to me.

BARBARA FOX, Eagan, Minnesota

BLESSING FOR MOTHER AND CHILD

Loving God,
Bless this woman and the new life she has birthed into the world.
As she swaddles her baby, may she too be enfolded in Your unconditional, motherly embrace.
Precious these two lives, forever bonded to each other—and to You!
Amen

—JANET BRISTOW

T HIS SHAWL IS JUST RIGHT FOR A MOTHER TO

FROM
Janet Severi
Bristow

wrap herself and her child in while nursing, providing a private space for nursing or just cuddling. Consider making this shawl a bit longer so that it can easily drape around mother and baby. Note that fringe might not be a good idea for this shawl, but a nice crocheted border enhanced by a coordinating ribbon, adds just the right touch. And, of course, please select a yarn that can be machine washed and dried.

NURSING SHAWL

Skill Level
Easy

Finished Measurements
55 in long and 23 in wide

Yarn
- Bulky Weight Yarn (CYCA), approx 555 yd Blue
- Shawl shown in Bernat Baby Bouclé (97% acrylic/3% polyester; 180 yd/3.5 oz), 4 skeins #36922 Fancy Free

Trim
- 2 yd 1/4-in satin ribbon

Needles
- Size 11 straight or circular needles (or size needed to obtain gauge)
- Size J or K crochet hook

Gauge
- 9 sts and 17 rows = 4 in worked in pattern

DIRECTIONS
CO 57 sts.

Row 1: Work k3, p3 across.

Row 2: Work k3, p3 across, being sure to knit the purl stitches and purl the knit stitches as they face you.

Repeat Rows 1 and 2 until shawl reaches from fingertip to fingertip, or desired length. BO all sts.

FINISHING
With crochet hook, attach yarn on one end of shawl with a sc. Work edging as follows: *Sk 2 sts, work 5 dc in next st, sk 2 sts, sc in next st, repeat from * across. Repeat on other end. Weave satin ribbon through holes created by dc clusters and tie in a double knot at ends to secure.

Widthwise-Knit Shawl

THIS SIMPLE PATTERN IS KNIT lengthwise on circular needles, although it is easily made up widthwise as well. You simply knit three rows and then purl three rows. This creates a lovely shawl with a ridge effect and a nice drape. Any yarn will do. The shawl knitted lengthwise is knit in a worsted weight ribbon yarn; the shawl knit widthwise (at left) is made of a hand-dyed silk and wool yarn combined with a strand of silk and mohair yarn. This shawl is also knit with a technique known as "condo knitting," in which two different-size needles are used on every other row. The result is an open, lacy look with no extra effort. Have fun experimenting—the greater the difference in needle size, the lacier the effect.

FROM
Kathy Andreoli
West Hartford, Connecticut

THREEFOLD BLESSING SHAWL

Widthwise-Knit Shawl

Skill Level
Easy

Finished Measurements
60 in long and 19 in wide

Yarn
- Bulky Weight Yarn (CYCA 5), approx 600 yd Gold
- Shawl shown in Alchemy™ Yarns Synchronicity (50% Merino wool/50% silk; 110 yd/1.75 oz), 6 skeins #64C Hidden Place, and Alchemy Yarns Haiku (60% mohair/40% silk; 325 yd/0.875 oz), 2 skeins #67E Topaz, 1 strand of each held tog

Needles
- Sizes 10 and 15 straight or circular needles (or sizes needed to obtain desired effect, using condo knitting)

Gauge
- 12 sts and 15 rows = 4 in worked in pattern stitch

DIRECTIONS
With larger needle, CO 57 sts.

Alternating larger and smaller needle, knit 3 rows, purl 3 rows until shawl measures 60 in or desired length.

BO all sts.

Add macramé fringe, if desired.

THREEFOLD BLESSING SHAWL

Lengthwise-Knit Shawl

Skill Level
Easy

Finished Measurements
63 in long and 15½ in wide

Yarn
- Bulky Weight Yarn (CYCA 5) approx 600 yd Orange
- Shawl shown in Bernat Miami (100% acrylic; 81 yd/1.75 oz), 6 skeins #34714 Orangina

Needles
- Size 11 circular needles, at least 29 in long (or size needed to obtain gauge)

Gauge
- 14 sts and 18 rows = 4 in worked in pattern stitch

DIRECTIONS
CO 150 sts.

Knit 3 rows, purl 3 rows until shawl measures 18 in wide, or desired width.

BO all sts.

Add fringe if desired.

Lengthwise-Knit Shawl

What Are the Words?

Cate Rooney, 6 years old, is the granddaughter of my husband's twin sister, and a very dear little girl to me. She also has minimal change disease, which is a kidney disease that occurs in children. It's a treatable condition in most cases, though its effects are anything but "minimal." The tests and treatments can have serious side effects, are painful, and take a long time. When I heard about Cate's diagnosis, I wanted to do something for her. So I began making her a prayer shawl.

I showed Cate the start of her prayer shawl, and she wanted to watch me work on it. I told her the words I say to concentrate on the pattern and the prayers: "Creator loves Cate; Savior loves Cate; Sanctifier loves Cate" (for one set of three stitches) and "God the Father loves Cate; Son loves Cate; Holy Spirit loves Cate." I'll also simply say, "Faith, Hope, Love" (another set of three) or "Peace, Joy, Trust." I was grateful that Cate liked this shawl so much she wanted to make one herself. Her mom had yarn, I had needles, and her grandma had time to show her how.

The very next day, I got an urgent call from Cate's grandma: "What are the *words*?" she asked. I was somewhat confused until I finally realized that, for Cate, a necessary part of making her prayer shawl was asking for or feeling the presence of God. Knitting a prayer shawl simply wasn't complete without the prayer.

I don't know how far Cate got in her knitting (she is only 6, after all), but I do know that she sleeps with the prayer shawl I made her—though in San Diego, California, she hardly needs it for warmth. And shortly after she received it, she made me a drawing copying that prayer shawl in Magic Markers—a very special thank-you.

ANNIE BABSON, Montrose, California

THREEFOLD BLESSINGS

Give threefold blessings as you
Stitch, pray, and create.

Extend threefold blessings as you
Reach out, touch, and enfold,

Receive threefold blessings to
Fill, encourage, and inspire you
To do it all over again.

—JANET SEVERI BRISTOW

THIS SHAWL IS A WONDERFUL WAY TO USE up odds and ends of yarns left over from shawls or other projects. You can choose a color and use yarns only in shades of that color, or make up your own colorway (based on autumn or ocean colors, for example), or make a "crazy shawl" of sorts, using any colors you happen to have. For more fun, share yarns from the stashes of your friends or those in your prayer shawl group.

FROM
Janet Severi
Bristow

TRAVELING SHAWL

Skill Level
Easy

Finished Measurements
76 (84) in long and 17 in wide

Yarn
- Medium (CYCA 4) to Bulky (CYCA 5) yarns, approx 750 yd total of a variety of yarns: smooth, chenille, eyelash, ribbon, thick-and-thin, and so on (thinner yarns may be combined to achieve desired weight)
- Shawl shown in a variety of yarns

Needles
- Size 13 circular needle, at least 29 in long (or size needed to obtain gauge)

Gauge
- 10 sts and 20 rows = 4 in worked in pattern

DIRECTIONS
Before casting on, allow for a long-enough tail of yarn for a fringe (12 in or desired length). With yarn of choice, CO 130 (150).

Row 1: K3, p3 across. At end of row, fasten off yarn and cut, leaving a tail of yarn same length as that on opposite end.

Row 2: Attach a new yarn, leaving enough for a fringe. Knit the purl sts and purl the knit sts as they face you. At end of row, fasten off yarn and cut, leaving a tail of yarn same length as established fringe.

Work as established, attaching new yarn for each row and leaving a tail for fringe on both ends, until shawl is desired width. BO all sts.

FINISHING

After body of shawl is complete, go back and fill in any spaces in the fringe. Knot together in groups of 4 to 6 strands, if desired, or weave in ends and attach tassels to corners.

Tassel

Wrap yarn around an object (piece of cardboard, pack of cards) the same length as desired length of tassel. When finished, thread a length of yarn on a needle and slide it under the top wraps of the tassel. Tie tightly, and do not trim (use the strands to attach the tassel to the project). Slide a scissors blade under the bottom wraps and cut. Tie a second length of yarn around the tassel about $1/2$ in from the top and tie tightly. Trim the ends to tassel length.

Sisterhood of the Shawl

Inspired by the movie *The Sisterhood of the Traveling Pants*, my girlfriends and I wondered what article of clothing we could all share. Because we were of all shapes and sizes, pants were out of the question. One friend said that a prayer shawl would fit everyone. She was right.

Unbeknownst to anyone else at that time, one woman in our group was facing major surgery at the end of summer. When I found this out, I thought it would be a great idea if we all made a "traveling prayer shawl." We prayed for each other as we knit, especially for the first recipient of the shawl, for whom it was a surprise. We kept a journal while we were knitting to see where the shawl traveled that summer and to read everyone's thoughts and prayers as they knit it. We decided that, in the true spirit of a traveling shawl, this one would be shared by everyone in the group during her own time of need.

At the end of the summer, we gathered at the home of the friend who was scheduled for surgery and prayed with her. She was asked to find a ribbon to lace through the stitches of the shawl as her contribution to it and to write her feelings and prayers in the journal as well. Since then, two other women in the group have had a need for the shawl. And both have found it very comforting and empowering.

RUTH SPRONG, Manchester, Connecticut

FROM
Alice Beck
Christiana, Pennsylvania

THIS IS A GREAT PATTERN FOR SHAWL MAKERS wishing to learn the basic lace techniques of yarn over and knit two together. In this pattern—a variation on the Fan and Feather or Old Shale pattern—the combination of the two techniques results in a zigzag effect. In the first row, the yarn overs and decreases create the scalloped lace pattern, followed by a simple purl row and a simple knit row. Beginners may want to keep track of these rows as they go along.

Experiment with the yarn and needle size, if you wish, to get different effects. The very bulky hand-dyed yarn used here resulted in a thick, heavy shawl that we affectionately call a "bear." A worsted weight or slightly bulky yarn would create a lighter, lacier effect with size 11 or 13 needles.

ALICE'S LACE SHAWL

Skill Level
Intermediate

Finished Measurements
70 in long and 23 in wide

Yarn
• Super Bulky Weight (CYCA 6), approx 700 yd Red
• Shawl shown in Decadent Fibers Crème Puff (80% merino wool/20% mohair; 140 yd/8 oz), 5 skeins Red Hot Pepper

Needles
• Size 15 straight or circular needles (or size needed to obtain gauge)

Gauge
• 8 sts and 12 rows = 4 in worked in pattern

DIRECTIONS
CO 56 sts.

Row 1: *K1, k2tog, k4, yo, k1, yo, k4, k2tog twice, k4, yo, k1, yo, k4, k2tog, k1. Repeat from * once.

Row 2: Purl across.

Row 3: Knit across.

Repeat Rows 1–3 until shawl measures 70 in, or desired length. BO all sts.

FINISHING
If desired, add simple tassels to the point of each scallop, using two 18-in strands of yarn per tassel (there will be 5 on one side, 6 on the other). See page 27 for details.

A GLIMPSE OF HEAVEN

Our prayer shawls can be an aid to praying
as a cane is an aid for the lame.
They are like a hug from God,
our Heavenly Father.
These shawls touch Heaven to earth.
The warmth we feel is like a glimpse of what
being in Heaven would be like.
The glory of the Lord shines round about
you as you wrap it around you.
Our faith is strengthened as we pray more
often in this comfort.

—RUTH BEITELSPACHER
ABERDEEN, SOUTH DAKOTA

The Healer's Touch

In biblical times, one woman had but to touch the fringe of Jesus' garment to be healed. In troubled times, we need but to touch the fringes of our shawls and feel their blessings. They are a gift to us to help us prepare for our final walk. Followers of Jesus had to keep this faith hidden, so often when others were near they would draw outlines of fish in the sand as a secret symbol.

As I knit my prayer shawls, I like to lay the skeins of yarn on a stool to my left, as soon as the yarn can be pulled from the center without stress. Then a miracle happens. It is mysterious, as if light pushes through the skein's tunnel, and it is even brighter at my end of the skein. I pause and feel the presence of God as the yarn works through my hands and becomes a special prayer shawl for someone in need. The glory of God shines round about us and with the ones who receive and use their shawls.

I tell my friends who have received shawls because they are sick, or about to be married, or bereaved, or even in the process of selling a home and moving to an apartment to use the shawl in special quiet time. Praising God, giving thanks, even letting Jesus know your thoughts are ways of answering Jesus' call.

RUTH BEITELSPACHER
Aberdeen, South Dakota

KNITTING ABBREVIATIONS

approx	approximate(ly)
BO	bind off
CC	contrasting color
ch	chain (crochet)
CO	cast on
dc	double crochet
dec	decrease
k	knit
k1-b	knit 1 stitch in row below
kf&b	knit in the front and back of 1 stitch (increase)
k2tog	knit 2 stitches together
in	inch(es)
inc	increase
MC	main color
m1	make 1 stitch (increase)
oz	ounce(s)

p	purl
psso	pass slipped stitch over decrease)
p2tog	purl 2 stitches together (decrease)
RS	right side
sc	single crochet
sk	skip (crochet)
sl	slip
ssk	slip 1 stitch knitwise, slip 1 stitch knitwise, knit the 2 slipped stitches together (decrease)
st/sts	stitch/stitches
tog	together
WS	wrong side
yd	yard(s)
yo	yarn over

STANDARD YARN WEIGHTS

ACTUAL YARN	NUMBERED BALL	DESCRIPTION	STS/4 IN	NEEDLE SIZE
Superfine	1	Sock, baby, fingering	27–32	27–32 2.25–3.25 mm (U.S. 1–3)
Fine	2	Sport, baby	23–26	3.25–3.75 mm (U.S. 3–5)
Light	3	DK, light worsted	21–24	3.75–4.5 mm (U.S. 5–7)
Medium	4	Worsted, afghan, Aran	16–20	4.5–5.5 mm (U.S. 7–9)
Bulky	5	Chunky, craft, rug	12–15	5.5–8.0 mm (U.S. 9–11)
Super bulky	6	Bulky, roving	6–11	8 mm and larger (U.S. 11 and larger)

Look for these other THREADS Selects booklets at www.taunton.com and wherever crafts are sold.

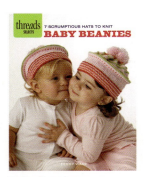

Baby Beanies
Debby Ware

EAN: 9781621137634
8 ½ x 10 ⅞, 32 pages
Product# 078001
$9.95 U.S., $11.95 Can.

Fair Isle Flower Garden
Kathleen Taylor

EAN: 9781621137702
8 ½ x 10 ⅞, 32 pages
Product# 078008
$9.95 U.S., $11.95 Can.

Fair Isle Hats, Scarves, Mittens & Gloves
Kathleen Taylor

EAN: 9781621137719
8 ½ x 10 ⅞, 32 pages
Product# 078009
$9.95 U.S., $11.95 Can.

Lace Socks
Kathleen Taylor

EAN: 9781621137894
8 ½ x 10 ⅞, 32 pages
Product# 078012
$9.95 U.S., $11.95 Can.

Colorwork Socks
Kathleen Taylor

EAN: 9781621137740
8 ½ x 10 ⅞, 32 pages
Product# 078011
$9.95 U.S., $11.95 Can.

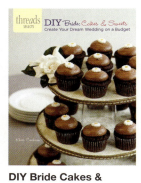

DIY Bride Cakes & Sweets
Khris Cochran

EAN: 9781621137665
8 ½ x 10 ⅞, 32 pages
Product# 078004
$9.95 U.S., $11.95 Can.

DIY Bride Beautiful Bouquets
Khris Cochran

EAN: 9781621137672
8 ½ x 10 ⅞, 32 pages
Product# 078005
$9.95 U.S., $11.95 Can.

Bead Necklaces
Susan Beal

EAN: 9781621137641
8 ½ x 10 ⅞, 32 pages
Product# 078002
$9.95 U.S., $11.95 Can.

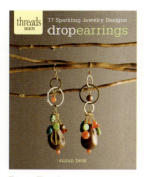

Drop Earrings
Susan Beal

EAN: 9781621137658
8 ½ x 10 ⅞, 32 pages
Product# 078003
$9.95 U.S., $11.95 Can.

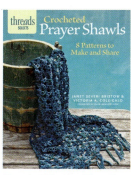

Crochet Prayer Shawls
Janet Severi Bristow & Victoria A. Cole-Galo

EAN: 9781621137689
8 ½ x 10 ⅞, 32 pages
Product# 078006
$9.95 U.S., $11.95 Can.

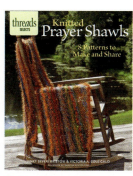

Knitted Prayer Shawls
Janet Severi Bristow & Victoria A. Cole-Galo

EAN: 9781621137696
8 ½ x 10 ⅞, 32 pages
Product# 078007
$9.95 U.S., $11.95 Can.

Shawlettes
Jean Moss

EAN: 9781621137726
8 ½ x 10 ⅞, 32 pages
Product# 078010
$9.95 U.S., $11.95 Can.